D0167234

When Your Child Isn't Doing Well in School

Ann Thiel, Ph.D.,
Richard Thiel, Ph.D.,
and Penelope B. Grenoble, Ph.D.

CONTEMPORARY
BOOKS

CHICAGO · NEW YORK

ACKNOWLEDGMENTS

Writing books and helping underachieving children find common cause in that both require a passionate dedication to teamwork. We are particularly indebted to Amy Reagin of UCLA and Jessica McRainey of the University of Colorado, who both did library research for this book, on top of their otherwise busy schedules. Without their long hours, this project would not have been the same.

We are also indebted to Barbara Stein, who labored at the typewriter evenings after having already worked a full day, and to a certain young teacher without whom, though he shall remain nameless, this book would have been quite impossible.

We dedicate this book especially to our own children: Geoffrey, an artist in New York; Nancy, a doctoral student in history at Johns Hopkins University;

Amy, who recently completed her degree at UCLA in mathematics, graduating with honors; Julie, a doctoral student and teaching assistant at the University of Wyoming; Liz, doggedly pursuing a career in acting; and Maria, currently a sophomore at California State University at Humboldt in art history.

We would also like to mention Lindsey and Craig Wallace, whose academic achievements have made us proud; Kara Michelle, making strong headway in the third grade; and finally, our godchild, Vanessa, looking out on a brand-new world with wonder and fascination in her twinkling blue eyes, and toward a future we will not see.

—RHT and AFT

Special thanks to Keshav Kamath for his help in preparing this manuscript and to Creighton Grenoble for computer assistance.

—PBG

CONTENTS

An Introduction to *ParentBooks That Work*

I t has been said that twenty-five-dollar words can be used to cover up twenty-five-cent ideas. In our increasingly technological society, jargon and complex language often confuse the meaning of information. This is particularly the case in the social and psychological sciences.

The "hard sciences" such as physics, chemistry, and biology have an advantage: there is little chance, for example, that a photon or a quark will be confused with something else.

In the human sciences, however, we have at least two problems with language. One is that the popular definition of a word such as *sex* or *intelligence* can differ considerably from the way a professional in the field might use it. Although we parents share a common pool of language with social scientists and teachers and therapists, words like *input* and *reinforcement, expectations* and *assessment*, mean one thing to parents and another to social science experts. Thus the danger that we will not understand each other is very real.

The human sciences' other language problem is jargon. A particular group of human scientists may develop obscure or seemingly incomprehensible language as a shortcut to communication among its members. Thus, jargon can be a roadblock when the experts try to talk to people outside their field.

The books in this series are the result of skillful collaboration between trained psychologists experienced in family and child development and a seasoned writer. The authors have strived to take twenty-five-dollar ideas and deliver them in language that is clear, concise, and most useful to you. In these six books, the emphasis is on presenting intelligent and practical ideas that you can use to help solve the age-old problems of child rearing.

This brings us to the very reason for these books. It might have occurred to you to ask, "Why should I rely on so-called experts when I can fall back on tradition and conventional wisdom? After all, the human race has survived well on what parents have taught children through the ages." Think about that for a moment. In the long history of human life on this planet, most of our energy has been spent in survival against the elements. It's only in most recent history that we've enjoyed the luxury to live, rather than simply survive. The fact is that the help and advice children need most nowadays has to do with a different level of survival in a world we've created ourselves, a complex world of rapid change.

Even though at moments nature can remind us of her often terrible wrath and power, most of our problems are still manmade. What we—parents and children both—have to learn is to deal with a reality that we have created ourselves.

In the bewildering array of cultures, creeds, and cross-purposes that are modern life, we need a special set of skills to live and be productive. Competition is an essential fact of life. Your child faces stress and pressure from society's expectations from the day he or she is born. To get through, your child needs the best help you can give.

The position of the professional expert is new and revered in our society. The expert is one of our cleverest inventions. Involved in the intense study of one problem or subject, the expert comes to know it better than anyone else. We trust the expert because we know that we don't have the time or ability to sort out everything ourselves. And, if the expert follows the best instincts of his profession, his high level of professional competence will serve you. By using the specialized knowledge of the expert, parents can face the difficult but practical problems of building a family and preparing their children to meet the demands of early childhood and elementary school.

Enlightened by this advice, we can give our children a healthy attitude and a better chance.

These concise and practical books deal with some of the most important issues in young children's lives today. They will help you to help your child and to feel good about your role as a parent. With this in mind, we dedicate this series to you.

Richard H. Thiel, Ph.D.
California State University

INTRODUCTION

The complex world of the twentieth century can be a frightening place to live and raise children. Parents facing such challenges as dual-career marriages, divided families, stepparenting, and single parenthood often find themselves overloaded by the demands of working and raising a family. Feelings of frustration, guilt, and anger often result as parents divide their time and energy amid complicated, and often conflicting, demands. But as difficult as coping with the modern world can be for adults, society also expects more from our children. Sometimes parents don't understand what this can do to a child.

Children, especially very young children who are facing their first experiences with preschool, kindergarten, or elementary school, can be even more highly sensitive than their parents to the pressures of their lives. Children experience the world on a more primitive, intuitive basis, and often feel stress and pressure much more than their parents. Futhermore, they are much less prepared for dealing with these effects. Loving our children, being emotionally involved with them, and having great hopes and desires for their happiness and success can often blind us to the problems they may be having as they move out of the home into the world. These problems multiply when your child crosses over that magic threshold—from the family into the "real" world, which for most children is symbolized by their first experiences in school.

Because of a variety of changes in our society in the past twenty years, the line of demarcation between home and school has become much less distinct. Children are often placed in day-care centers and preschools at a younger age and certainly in greater numbers. This means that they begin to feel the crush of social pressure at a younger age, when they may not be able to cope with it. Sometimes problems within the family loom so large that the child cannot exercise his best efforts. School becomes a challenge he cannot meet.

It is always difficult to generalize, because the age and stage at which children accomplish developmental tasks vary, but many children may find themselves unprepared for this accelerated push forward. Although there are a number of indications of a child's successful completion of the developmental challenges appropriate to his age, none is more obvious—or more anxiously awaited and carefully scrutinized—than his reactions to school. In this regard, school refers less to preschool or day-care than to the formal academic program that will be part of your child's life from roughly age five to twenty-two (assuming he goes to either college or technical school).

It is at this stage that children begin to reach out beyond the family and to experience the larger environment, with its own demands and rewards. When your child enters school he comes face to face with the expectations of other adults and must actively interact with other children. Unfortunately, it is at this very formative stage that many parents suddenly become acutely aware of their children's progress. When children are limited primarily to the home and family environment where their primary concern is pleasing their parents, it's easy to overlook behavior problems and to dismiss signs that a child may be lagging behind. It's easy to think that such things will be ironed out when the child grows up and goes to school—as if going to school provides some special formula. You should realize, however, that the way your child reacts to the world and its challenges has more to do with what *you* teach him and how *you* react to him in those precious years of early childhood than all his experiences in all the years ahead. *The process of growth and development starts at birth, not in preschool or kindergarten.*

The great sadness is that often it is the brightest and most capable of our children who find themselves experiencing difficulty when they enter the world of school. Often these children come from homes where parents themselves are high achievers and expect a lot of their children. Until recently this was a perplexing problem. Thanks to dedicated researchers and therapists, however, we are finally coming to understand that this actually happens to many children and that there are common causes. Happily, this has led us to understand what parents can do to help a child foundering on the shoals of academic achievement.

Our culture teaches us that the people who work the hardest will be most successful. While there is no mistaking the role of motivation in accomplishment, no one can keep trying in the face of constant defeat. Skill, talent, and ability, if not adequately guided, have a slim chance of being developed to the fullest. Your child's skill and ability need guidance, practice, and encouragement for him to be able to develop them to the fullest. He should also understand some of the challenges he'll face in competing in the world as well as the fact he will sometimes make mistakes.

Intelligence and motivation are not the only reasons for academic success. Likewise, failure to achieve in school should never be viewed solely as lack of trying. Success in school is important to your child's sense of worth. A child who continually fails in school will have a hard time in life. This is a tragedy for the individual and also for society, which is deprived of a vital source of talent.

And so it is that, in the short scope of this volume, we have chosen to focus on what the academic world calls *underachievers*—the child of average or above-average intelligence who for a variety of reasons is not doing well in school. (Parents who suspect that their child has severe learning disabilities or suffers from physiological problems are advised to consult the large body of literature on these subjects and to seek professional help.) What we offer here is advice and specific recommendations for the parent whose child is not doing well in school. The material contained in this book is designed to help you make the most of your child's talents and the opportunities available to him in his school system. Our goal is also to help you. You are your child's most important resource. It's important that you understand the role you play as a parent and how your behavior can affect your child's future success. Although we are speaking primarily of children who, for various reasons, are consistently working below their capacity and potential, the same advice can be applied if your child has an occasional problem mastering a subject or loses interest in school.

As in all books in this series, a child is typically referred to as he; please remember that we are thinking of your daughter also. Her successful completion of an academic career is as vital and important as her brother's.

Part I
All Children Are
Not Created Equal

It is the opinion of educator Benjamin Bloom that 95 percent of students enrolled in U.S. schools today have the basic ability to master the existing curriculum—not just pass but master it. That means your child probably has the ability to learn what's being taught and how to use it to get what he wants in life. Bloom's research indicates that children who are average or above-average in intelligence—which is most children—are capable of learning and applying the curriculum in our schools today, given sufficient exposure and adequate practice. (It's a matter of common sense that this material should be presented in a way that makes sense to children and relates to their interests and needs.)

In many schools, however, problems due to overcrowded classes, insufficient teacher preparation, and budget restraints place the burden of learning on the student. Often there just are not enough hours in a day for a teacher to spend more than a few classroom minutes with each student, let alone be able to offer personal instruction. As children move from elementary school to junior high and high school, the time spent in one-on-one instruction often diminishes further.

There is no doubt that all children can benefit from more teacher-student interaction, but for the underachieving student, individual instruction is a must. Often by the time the problems of such children are diagnosed, they have fallen very far behind. The child has simply spent too much unproductive classroom time; has missed basic skills, especially language and reading and will lack basic information on which he can build.

While the problems of an underachiever may start in the home, deficiencies in the school system may compound the problem. This doesn't mean that the reason children don't do well in school is because schools are bad or curriculum is wrong. You should realize, however, that American education is designed to offer educational opportunities to the largest possible segment of society. This means that how and what we teach is geared to average children, who pass through it. Children who have severe learning problems or are exceptionally intelligent, or those who do not respond to the conventional classroom may find little meaning in school.

FACTORS THAT AFFECT ACADEMIC PROGRESS

Even if your child is lucky enough to be placed in a private school where the student-teacher ratio is lower and opportunity for learning is greater, both you and your underachieving child may have to assume greater responsibility in meeting the challenges of school. Often good intentions fall short of the effort needed to remedy the problem of underachievement. As with all childhood problems, the earlier they are recognized, the better, and the greater the effort to remedy the problem, the faster results will come.

Since the problem frequently starts in the home, you should take the time to evaluate your family life to see whether it may be affecting your child in a negative way. The following are a number of factors that may exist in your child's life and affect the academic progress of an underachiever.

Negative Parent-Child Interaction

Parents of underachieving children often feel frustrated, defeated, guilty, or angry. They don't understand their child's problems and feel incapable of dealing with them. Anger and frustration can be turned inward—at the parents themselves—or outward toward the child. In either case, both parents and child lose. The underchiever often feels isolated and outcast, as if the world's approval is hopelessly withdrawn from him. He knows that he is not meeting the standards. He knows he is not like other children, and often feels isolated from the world. Each of us requires some degree of approval from other people for the sake of our self-worth. Success in school during the early stages of life provides this primary form of approval.

Take the case of Frederick, for example. Freddy

was born into an affluent, two-career family. His father was the president of an electronics firm, his mother a lawyer. When Freddy was born, his mother made arrangements with the law firm to take some of her work home, enabling her to spend more time with her child. As Freddy grew, he was enrolled in nursery school, and his mother went back to work full-time. His nursery school teacher noticed that Freddy was not as lively as the other children, nor as developed in his play. He could not use toys, for example, or coordinate his movements well enough to play with the other children. Nor was he outgoing. He would sit and watch other children playing, his mouth agape, a dull expression on his face.

Despite the fact Freddy was diagnosed by school authorities as slightly mentally retarded, he was allowed to enroll in regular classes and was unfortunately promoted through the elementary grades. Compounding his intellectual problems was his poor muscle coordination, which showed little if any improvement over the preschool years. Freddy was finally referred to therapy. His parents were beside themselves about what to do and were frustrated and upset.

As part of therapy, it was confirmed that Freddy was not suffering from brain damage or problems with his nervous system. What did come out of the emotional therapy sessions was that Freddy was suffering from lack of attention from his parents. Though his mother had arranged to work at home, she actually paid little attention to him. Freddy's father also ignored his son; the child was isolated and alone. He had little if any opportunity to use his body or observe and practice kinds of movements children learn through play and other physical contact with their parents.

To help Freddy, the whole family entered therapy. Once they understood Freddy's problems and their role, his parents rose to the occasion and cooperated thoroughly. They both cut back on their work. His father arranged a four-day work week. His mother cut down the amount of work she brought home. Working with the therapist, Freddy's parents also made arrangements to take Freddy out of school one day a week, and one or the other or both of them would spend the whole day with him, playing, talking, even just shopping together or taking short trips. The therapist instructed the family in the need to communicate with each other and how they might do it. His mother, who had taught school for a short time before going to law school, even tutored Freddy in subjects where he was weakest. Mostly, however, his parents gave him love, attention, and time.

Gradually he began to turn around. His mother's tutoring helped him to make up for some of the skills he hadn't acquired in school. His father started a program of sports and physical activities with his son. Slowly Freddy was able to improve until he was finally able to work up to grade level and move on with his class. As he progressed, it became apparent that Freddy was a very bright child with exceptional ability in science. He distinguished himself in high school—in a class of four thousand students, he graduated in the top 10 percent of his class and from there went on to college.

Freddy, of course, was not mentally retarded; nor was he "stupid"—although he had carried both labels throughout his early elementary school years. Nor had his parents intended to neglect him; they were simply so caught up in their own lives that they couldn't see what was happening to their child, or how they were helping to cause it. Freddy's case is severe. Less dramatic situations are far more common and, unfortunately, because they are less dramatic, often continue and worsen as the child grows up. Freddy was diagnosed and the situation corrected when he was young, and the solution to his problems was relatively easy—although it did require that his parents rearrange their lifestyle. In many cases children who have problems similar to Freddy's are left to struggle through school, to the continued frustration of themselves and their parents—and the school system.

Whether your child can meet the standards is a matter of the level of his self-esteem—what he thinks of himself and his abilities. Likewise, the level of his self-esteem will affect how he does in school. A child who has little success in school isn't likely to feel good about himself and may eventually just give up. He'll be depressed, appear listless, and have little drive. Unable to compete with other children's behavior, he may give up and withdraw to his own world. Such children often are the targets in school systems because teachers and administrators can't help them and are frustrated. A teacher faced with a full classroom will necessarily be nervous about the presence of an underachieving child. He is just one additional burden, especially if the school system isn't set up to handle such problems or doesn't have programs the child can be referred to for help.

Since he is a negative presence in the classroom, he may be a source of anger and anxiety in the home. Parents of underachievers may develop a negative or nonnurturing attitude toward their underachieving children, especially if the family has high standards for academic and personal achievement. This contributes to the child's sense of isolation and causes further withdrawal.

For the underachiever, self-esteem is a Catch-22 situation. A child with low self-esteem will feel defeated and won't try to achieve—but if he doesn't try, there is no possibility for him to feel better. The only way to feel good about his capabilities is to try them out and find they're OK. But a child already racked with a sense of failure is unlikely to continue trying. In this way, a child's initial academic experiences can be crucial, especially if he comes from a disadvantaged or confused family. Perhaps his parents are divorced or both parents work. Either way, he is likely to have problems.

Social Stigma

An additional problem an underachieving child often faces is the stigma that may develop as a result of his academic capabilities. This is especially true in school systems that attempt to group children by ability and future life plans. A child who does not do well in his earliest school years may become "branded." Aside from the social difficulties this causes, it can also be a label that the child will come to believe. If a child tests bright but doesn't get much reinforcement at home and is placed in a highly achieving group of children, he may be lost and disoriented. He may withdraw academically and socially, or may feel isolated and inept by the group's standards.

Melody, for example, was chosen as part of a select group of college-bound students in an advanced school system. For these students the curriculum and teachers were more demanding, and the pace was much faster. Her parents, neither of whom were college-educated, failed to understand the significance of their daughter's special placement. Instead of reinforcing her efforts, they projected the subtle message that she did not really belong in this elite group—that her placement had been a fluke. Although Melody fought her parents' negative attitude, she began to find it more and more difficult to maintain the academic standards required of her and eventually asked to be placed in a lower group. Her parents immediately expressed disappointment and frustration at her failure to succeed. Melody fell behind because she unconsciously felt more comfortable achieving below the level of her capabilities; it was an easier way of dealing with the anxiety induced by her parents.

You may be surprised by a 1970 study published in the *Harvard Education Review* that indicates that, within the first eight days of school, children are classified into groups within the school environment—groupings that are likely to follow them through their school career and maybe through life. Worse is the news that children are not usually grouped by performance, but by teachers' expectations for achievement and accomplishment for children at a given age and skill level. It is not the label that becomes so much of a problem, but your child's internalization of his ability as reflected by his place in the system. Once teachers have classified children, they seldom reevaluate their opinions. Dr. Howard Garber, a veteran researcher in the field, concludes in his 1979 study, "The amount of harm being done today by teachers and educators steeped in the notion of the irreversibility of development and diminished potential in the disadvantaged child has major implications for the blunting of even the most effective educational program."

The same report suggests that many so-called underachieving—or what Garber calls disadvantaged—children are inhibited from succeeding in school because they are continually exposed to negative educational experiences. Frustration and failure are their constant companions. This lack of positive feedback, the report concluded, was a more important factor than the absence of academic stimulation. As adults, we well know the effects of positive reinforcement, of how rewards for past effort can cause us to try harder. It is a fact of human nature that as children are encouraged, they will strive harder and with increased effort. Unfortunately, it is also true that children who do not fit the conventional standards of success are often outcasts.

Sex-Role Expectations

Traditional expectations of sex roles also have a complex influence on underachievers. Various studies have shown, for example, that boys outnumber girls as underachievers by a ratio varying from 3:1 to 6:1. Our expectations for boys and girls can often contribute to underachievement. The effect on female children can be disastrous, because it is often expected that girls will be underachievers both in the classroom and at home. On the other hand, the effect on boys, though more subtle, can be just as bad. A little girl may be allowed to fall short of her best, because she is "Daddy's little girl" or "Mommy's precious." A boy, however, may find himself feeling overwhelmed by the expectation that he achieve or surpass his parents' and teachers' expectations.

It seems impossible in this day and age that sex-role expectations should be important, especially since so many children are raised in dual-career families or by single parents who must work and take care of a family. How can a career mother, for instance, allow her daughter to be a dependent, passive person when she is out in the trenches every day? Think of the conflicting message the young child is receiving: mother has the obligations of going to work every day, while I have no demands made on me to take responsibility for myself.

FURTHER UNDERSTANDING THE UNDERACHIEVER

Probing still deeper into the causes of underachievement, a Harvard team, H. Krouse and Helene J. Krouse, has assembled a theory of scholastic underachievement. The Krouses identified three major characteristics of underachievers:

Weakness in Academic Skills

Not surprisingly, underachieving children will show a weakness in basic academic skills such as reading, note taking, basic math procedures, test-taking strategies, and study skills.

Take the case of Sarah, for example. Sarah was the eight-year-old daughter of a jeweler. The entire family was very achievement-oriented. Both older brothers had done very well scholastically, and Sarah was expected to follow in their footsteps. Sarah, however, was not adhering to the program. She was referred for therapy because she could not complete her third-grade long division assignments. Her teacher was concerned that Sarah's problems were the result of a short attention span. Because of her frustration with Sarah's lack of progress, her teacher lowered her expectations for the child and labeled her an underachiever. Interestingly enough, Sarah's academic problems were not reflected in her social interactions. She was very social and was heavily involved in extracurricular events.

Sarah's therapy began with an assessment of her skills level, and it was immediately discovered that she didn't know her multiplication tables, which meant that it was impossible for her to make the leap from multiplication to division. Thus began the first step of learning multiplication so she could do division. A conference with Sarah's teacher produced a strategy whereby the teacher would provide Sarah with step-by-step tasks and reward her for achieving each step along the way. Overburdened with her family's expectations for her and her brothers' success, Sarah had been attempting to leap to the end result instead of patiently learning the layers of skills she needed in order to succeed.

Your child's progress or lack of progress is easily measured by evaluating his schoolwork. A check of a math workbook will give you an idea of the number of problems completed, with and without error. Spelling progress can be measured in the same manner. Bear in mind that success rate and error rate are both important. A child who makes no mistakes but completes very few problems has not adequately mastered the task. Mastery requires automatic response and recall so that the child can build on his current skills. It is important to realize that many academic tasks need to be "overlearned." Even when a child can complete the assignment with one hundred percent accuracy, further training and study may still be helpful.

Poor Social Skills

Underachieving children will have poor social skills and self-control. They'll have trouble judging the worth of what they do and planning how to do it. Take Larry, for example. Larry was a very thin and short ten-year-old who failed both academically and socially. He was brought to therapy by his parents, who had some idea of his problem but no idea of how to solve it. It seemed that Larry lagged behind the rest of his classmates because he could never get himself organized to do the work. It took a conference with the teacher and several therapy sessions with the parents to determine that Larry's strategy of being disorganized was a cover for the fears he had about his abilities. Both his parents and his teacher felt that Larry had an acute need to feel capable before he could achieve success. By never being organized enough to try, he never had to face the challenge of whether or not he could succeed.

A program was developed whereby Larry was forced to become organized by virtue of the fact that he was forced to accomplish his work. Larry's teacher began to require that specific tasks be completed in a specific amount of time—such as twenty-five short division problems within a five-minute drill. The teacher used a stopwatch and kept a daily record of Larry's progress, providing him precise feedback on what he'd done. The results were amazing. The more precise the feedback, the greater the improvement in Larry's performance. Likewise, Larry's parents were told when reviewing multiplication tables with him each night. Again the results were amazing. Success began to breed success.

Emotional Distractions

Underachievers will frequently have what are called emotional-psychological blocks. Fear and anxiety can inhibit a child from doing well on a test, even though he knows the subject. A child who has been isolated and alone may think he's not able to make friends and thus won't try. Fear of failing is very powerful. Actually, the child has already failed and will continue to fail.

Freddy suffered from these difficulties, as did Denise, a beautiful fifth-grader with big dark eyes and dark hair. Denise got along well with other children and enjoyed playing with them. She seemed to be a happy child who had experienced a normal early childhood. One day, however, Denise simply took it upon herself to leave school in the middle of the morning and was found wandering across the street. She was taken to the principal's office, and the ensuing scene seemed inexplicable, given her usual good behavior.

It turned out that Denise was frantic and hysterical about a test on decimals and percentages she had to take for the second time later that day. The retake was necessary because she had failed the first time the test was given. When questioned further, Denise maintained that she didn't know why she had failed or what she was supposed to do to succeed. She had received no precise feedback from the teacher. In the course of her conversation with the teacher and the principal, she asked if she was stupid or, as her father had put it, incompetent. The little girl had received a variety of input, all unspecific, which was so confusing to her that she just wanted to escape.

Denise was referred to a school district therapist, who helped unravel some of her problems. First, her father had been a successful athlete in school and had a strong sense of competition. When he heard that his daughter had been one of only a few to fail a test and had to retake it, he played the only role he knew—that of the coach at halftime in a losing game. He told Denise that there was no reason she should fail, that she had what it took, and that he expected her to go back and pass the test. However, he didn't offer any suggestions about how she was supposed to do this. He had not intended to be harsh with his daughter and had, in fact, thought he was doing the right thing. Unfortunately, Denise's teacher was not much more help than her father. Denise was part of a large class of students who were expected to do well. In reality the math skills required of them were somewhat advanced for their age group. These things had not, however, been explained to Denise or to her parents. She did not realize that she was actually in an advanced class and both she and her parents believed that Denise was failing in the basics.

The therapist worked with Denise's father and teacher and showed them how to encourage Denise and be precise in what they wanted her to do and how to do it. They were taught to reward even Denise's smallest steps toward improvement. Denise was lucky in that she came from a very loving, close family. Her mother had died when she was only a baby, but the extended family was still close and available to her. Denise had the love and support of grandparents, uncles, aunts, and cousins. Eventually, she was able to focus on success and duplicate that performance. For example, on the test she had failed, Denise actually had missed only a handful more problems than had the passing students, and she had completed more than half of the problems correctly. If the teacher had highlighted the work done correctly, Denise would have been able to understand the right and wrong way of doing the problems.

Abstract understanding is one of the last levels of intellectual development. You need to talk to your child in ways that he understands and that are meaningful to him.

BREAKING THE CYCLE OF UNDERACHIEVEMENT

It is not so much that the things just described *cause* underachievement but that it is predictable they will *develop* in the underachieving child. As we have seen, these factors may result from early academic experience or from difficulties at home, including neglect; they may also result from social trauma such as loss of a parent or death or divorce. As was noted previously, the difficulty is that underachievement can be a never-ending cycle. A child with poor skills will not be able to learn and will probably have no friends nor benefit from the care and concern of teachers and other adults. Without some kind of encouragement, he will feel his self-esteem slip to the point where it becomes impossible for him to extend himself to try.

As frustrating as the problems are for a child who isn't doing well in school, there is more hope today than ever before. New attitudes and improved teaching methods have emerged. Research in education and in related fields of psychology has begun to unravel the mysteries of how we actually learn. With this new information and ongoing work in this area, underachieving children no longer need to resign themselves to the life of class "bonehead." There are specific things that educators and parents can do to improve a child's performance in school, regardless of how poorly he has been doing. The situation *can* be evaluated and corrected.

In a review of the recent literature on under-achievement in the *Community Home and School Gazette*, L. F. Lowenstein summarized factors that can enhance a child's potential for the future. Specifically the recommendations include:

• *Identify underachieving children as early as possible.* Parents and teachers often put off acknowledging a child's problems out of fear of the repercussions. They chase down the path toward long years of testing and/or therapy and neglect the obvious factors in their life. It is wise, therefore, to confront the possibility that your child's problems in school are real, whether because of a faulty school system, inadequate resources, or conflicts in values between your child and his teacher. The longer your child wastes time *not* learning, the more time and effort you and the child will have to make to help catch up. Childhood is full of enough problems without having to cope with feelings of being left behind.

• *Plan how to help.* Once the problem is diagnosed, an organized course of action should be put in place. This may involve individual or family therapy. It may require some alteration in lifestyle on the part of the parent or family, or a look at family values and expectations. It will almost always mean an expenditure of time and effort by both parents and child. With severely underachieving children—those who are performing two levels or more below grade level as defined by the local school system—professional help will definitely be required. At this stage the child's self-esteem will have suffered so much that he will need professional guidance and care to recover.

• *Provide individual tutoring.* In doing so, you will be affording your child the amount of time and practice he needs to master the required academic tasks. You should not take these decisions upon yourself, however. A thorough examination of your child's strengths and weaknesses should be completed before you hire a tutor. And you should make sure that not only is the tutor qualified but that there is a good personality match between tutor and child. Selecting a tutor is part of a plan and should not be undertaken without guidance from a professional.

• *You should receive counseling about how you may best help your child, regardless of whether you are or your child is involved in therapy.* There are often problems in the family that are either so deeply embedded or so obvious that you are not aware of them and how they affect your child. They may be patterns of family interaction, conflicts in values about achievement, or even the physical aspects of the home environment. Whatever it is, if you haven't corrected it by now, you will need help discovering what it is and how best to cope.

• *Use incentives and reinforcement.* You and your child's teachers should strive for positive interactions (which, of course, may frequently mean ignoring behavior that isn't up to par or might trigger a negative reaction).

Research also suggests—and it is generally considered true among enlightened therapists—that drug therapy, which has in the past been used routinely with underachieving children, seems to provide no long-lasting, beneficial results. This is particularly important if your child has been classified as hyperactive—a diagnosis that is becoming increasingly suspect. Young children who act out in school are less often truly hyperactive than frustrated with the school or home environment. You should carefully consider all other options before resorting to drug therapy. It is most often the case that drugs treat the symptoms of the problem, leaving the actual problem untreated. Drugs may initially relieve the annoying behavior, but the cause will remain and may continue to grow worse.

One point that cannot be overemphasized is the advantage of early identification and correction of underachievement. As with most childhood problems, failure to achieve academically can be resolved most easily at the outset, before a consistent pattern has been established in the child's mind and behavior. You should watch for indications of it throughout your child's academic career, because a failure in elementary school often does not become an obvious problem until the adolescent years. Frequently the problem begins early in school as little more than an inability to grasp a few concepts. As the child continues in school, however, the small deficit is never made up. Several years down the line, a huge gap seems to open—one that began as a mere hairline crack.

Furthermore, if underachievement problems are not taken care of before your child reaches adolescence, you can be almost certain that the more intense and immediate problems of that age will aggravate the situation and make it difficult, if not impossible, to correct the problem. In this crucial stage of life, small failures in school can take on nightmarish proportions, leading to other problems. A child who might otherwise breeze through the challenges of the teen years may, for lack of self-esteem because of a failure of scholastic achievement, turn to drugs or alcohol and tune out entirely. Adolescents have great potential for social and personal fulfillment, but they have equal potential for behavior that is personally and socially destructive. Though achievement in school will not ensure that adolescence will be trouble-free, it will be one less factor in an already loaded equation.

You have more influence over your child's development than any other outside factor. You must establish your role as an effective parent early. The extent to which you will be able to maintain a positive influence over your high-school-age child's conduct is directly attributable to the amount and quality of the care and guidance you provided earlier. Though teachers and tutors may provide some help, you and the positive steps you take will ultimately make the difference.

It is therefore important that your child have the full benefit of strong support at home from the earliest years of his life. Before the age of five, a child's experience is primarily in the home, with parents, who serve as the child's role models. The quality of parent-child interaction is a primary source of self-esteem. If your child has had positive interactions before entering school and has received your encouragement and love, school will present an exciting challenge. If your child's efforts at creativity have met with approval, he will be more likely to welcome the challenges of early school years with enthusiasm. And if support from you and your child's teachers continues, your children should do well.

In the early years your love, encouragement, and approval are more important than attempts to teach a very young child advanced skills such as basic arithmetic or reading. Children go through stages of development, and generally speaking, it is better to allow them to progress by their own timetable, rather than attempt to speed up the process. Your child's happiness and enjoyment of playful, creative activities in the early preschool years will help him enter school ready to respond to the challenges of the classroom and with the self-esteem to face them constructively.

The discussion of the stages of childhood growth presented in the companion book *Creating a Good Self-Image in Your Child* may be helpful to you in assessing your child's age-related capabilities and in developing activities appropriate to specific growth periods.

Part II
Some Guidelines for Recognizing Underachievement

Sociologist Robert K. Merton has a theory about how we choose social goals and our means for attaining them. His framework, by now somewhat of a classic, allows for several possible social orientations. The first is the option to pursue socially accepted goals by socially accepted means. If you needed a new automobile, for example, you would work and save money toward its purchase. The second involves the pursuit of the same socially sanctioned goal but uses socially unacceptable means. Instead of saving to buy an automobile, a person might steal one. Finally, there is a third approach, with implications for the subject of this book. In this category we find individuals who neither aspire to the usual, socially accepted goals nor use socially accepted means to obtain what they do want. These are people who have in effect given up on dreams of living normal lives by normal means—people such as drug users, who are a threat to themselves and to others. They are caught in a kind of "Twilight Zone" of their own making.

Such people are often difficult to cope with—and as difficult to treat and reform—because the usual motivations do not impel them. In turn, society reacts by rejecting them. When efforts are made to help them, the methods employed are generally harsh and mechanistic, resulting more often in a change of symptoms rather than a substantive personality change.

Underachieving children are subject to some of the same reactions experienced by this third category of social misfits—not necessarily because they are likely to wind up in destructive lifestyles, but because a pattern is established early in their life. Their behavior sets them apart from other children. Their motivations are misunderstood, and the methods taken to bring them in line are sometimes harsh and mechanistic.

The reality of underachieving children is that society seems to have excluded them from attaining normal goals by any means. In fact, underachievers are not expected to achieve or do well at those things that are seemingly required of everyone else. This implied judgment becomes a self-fulfilling prophecy. If you don't believe you'll succeed, you won't. Yet the means for reversing these tendencies are available in the home and the family, where the most crucial factors of influence reside. The first step is for you to recognize the problem.

FACTORS OF UNDERACHIEVEMENT

The label *underachiever* has become one of the buzzwords of contemporary society, a familiar catchall phrase that almost always is negative. Whether we are speaking of a co-worker whose lack of attention to his job makes ours more difficult or someone who is just too laid back and doesn't make adequate use of his intelligence and experience, we are most often implying negativity. But to think of an underachieving child in negative terms is a grave mistake.

In defining the problem, we are forced to use its designated label, but please be aware that we do so without judgmental negativity. Our concern is that the term *underachiever* carries with it the implication that the child has a choice, that he has actively chosen *not* to complete an assignment, *not* to live up to his potential. As we have suggested thus far, it is the underlying premise of this book that such a child is in no way exercising a choice, but actually becomes victimized by forces that he is unable to control.

There are two aspects to the concept of achievement: first, accomplishment or completion of a task or a goal; and second, development of a skill or capability. Underachieving children suffer from failure in both senses. They are faced with the reality that they may never accomplish what they think they would like to do, and worse, they will never be able to realize their goals in life. Likewise, they feel that they will never be able to acquire the required skills or the necessary capacity to consummate their potential, and in turn reach their goals.

In this sense, our definition of underachievement is both broader and more limited than what you may have traditionally considered. We are not speaking only of the child who is not in the top of his class (although, strictly speaking, given that child's level of intelligence and capability, he may be an underachiever), nor of a child who may not do well in a particular subject because his interests and/or aptitudes might not lie in that area. *Rather, we are referring here to the child who consistently works at a level below his capability, often to the point where his behavior attracts the attention of his teacher or other adults in his academic environment, as well as his parents.* (We are confining our attention here to the academic part of the school environment, exclusive of extracurricular activities.) Each child is different, yet all share at least one basic commonality: performance significantly below grade level, indicated by such factors as intelligence (as measured by the Stanford-Binet Intelligence Scale) and the ability to accomplish required tasks.

When an otherwise normal child cannot complete assignments in the classroom, something is wrong. Lest you jump to conclusions, however, you are advised to investigate whether the problem has an obvious cause. Perhaps the reason is as simple as your child needing glasses, or his suffering from some other kind of physiological problem. Or maybe it is a personality clash between the child and his teacher, a common and frustrating problem that the correct type of parental interaction can solve. If you have considered all such possibilities, then you should evaluate your child in terms of the following items. These characteristics are often symptoms of underlying problems that can lead to underachievement.

An Underachieving Child Frequently Has a Short Attention Span

If your child has difficulty concentrating on specific tasks for any sustained length of time, especially if he shows little interest in taking that task to its conclusion, it is likely that the difficulty is more than boredom. If your child cannot stay with one activity for more than several minutes before rushing off to something else, it may be that he is really not interested in what he is supposed to be doing or that he avoids completion because he is afraid that his performance will not be up to par. He may begin one activity only to almost immediately abandon it for another. His academic and extracurricular life may be littered with hastily conceived and then abandoned projects. Although completion anxiety is often a reason for short attention span, it may also be that your child lacks the skills to perform the task at hand. Or it may be that the task is boring and uninteresting to him and fails to engage his interest.

Take the case of Marley, a seven-year-old foster child, who was recommended for therapy because of a reading problem in school. His foster parents were an affluent older couple who gave Marley plenty of attention and the best of everything. He was enrolled in a good private school, where his reading deficiency was immediately diagnosed and tutoring was initiated. The principal also recommended therapy to help determine other possible causes for Marley's reading problems. His symptoms were not uncommon for many young children today: He tired quickly while looking at print and could not maintain attention to a reading task for more than a few minutes at a time. It appeared almost as if he could not read at all. He would gaze off into a corner of the room after haltingly reading a few lines. In tests on lists of words for word recognition, he was able to work through one list and part of another, but he quickly became fatigued. Even if a word he previously recognized recurred in the next list, Marley would misidentify it. *Here*, *there*, and *where* were all the same to him, even though he was very bright for his age and had a large spoken vocabulary, both in usage and recognition.

The therapist discovered in the first session that Marley had never been read to and that reading had not been modeled in the home as a recreational activity. Additionally, it was determined that Marley spent the majority of his free time watching TV. His parents had a VCR and a rather extensive video-cassette library, which Marley was free to use. He could remember lines from movies and sequences of action amazingly well and had analyzed the movies more than one would expect of a child so young. Even though tests indicated his IQ was extremely high, he was in the lower third of his class.

It was further discovered that the time Marley did have with his parents, particularly his father, was frequently spent in front of the television watching videos. In fact, they spent hours together watching and carrying on a running discussion of what was happening, which explained Marley's attentiveness, retention, knowledge, and enthusiasm for what he saw on the screen. Ironically, when his parents read for recreation or work, they would go off to another part of the house. His father often spent hours working in his study, and his mother would read in another room while Marley and her husband watched movies together. Neither of them had thought they might be depriving the boy by their actions. They had in fact judiciously kept their "personal" intellectual behaviors, such as reading, separate from time spent as a family.

On the therapist's recommendation, both parents began to participate in a home reading program with Marley while limiting his time watching TV videos to an hour a day and only those shows or movies his parents approved. Marley's parents read to him at least an hour a day and sometimes as many as three, at first in shorter installments. During all of their sessions, Marley would look on while one of them read. Every few lines, they might ask him to read a line or a word. They started with Dr. Seuss books, then *Winnie the Pooh* (Marley had seen the movie) and other A. A. Milne books, which delighted the boy, and progressed through *Paddington Bear* to *Alice in Wonderland* in a matter of months. The time spent reading was relaxing for the family, and Marley's father was able to carry on similar conversations with his son as he had while watching TV.

In the long run, Marley's unaccustomed eyes adapted to looking at print. He began reading more with his parents and took more interest in reading at school. He began reading cartoons his teacher hung on the wall. He became interested in books around the classroom and the house, reading the spines, taking them down from the shelves, reading a little to see what they might be about. Marley and his parents began reading the J. R. R. Tolkien books, beginning with *The Hobbit*. Marley's vocabulary, word recognition, comprehension, and overall endurance for reading had progressed incredibly in less than a year.

The symptom of a short attention span is particularly telling if you also notice that while your child may be regularly inattentive to schoolwork, particularly in-class assignments, he spends a lot of time in activities outside of school. Children who can't work math problems may do the math for carpentry or mechanical projects. A child who shows no interest in science out of a book may collect specimens of plants or insects, or may observe the habits of birds or animals with great attention and accuracy. Great thinkers sometimes exhibit this paradox of attention span. Albert Einstein, who developed the theory of relativity and devoted himself to theoretical physics, was so uninterested and incapable of performing in school that his teachers and his parents thought he might be mentally retarded. If your child lacks the patience to stick with an assignment, it does not necessarily mean he lacks intelligence, but it may signify potential underachievement problems.

An Underachiever May Show Immature Behavior

If your child acts immaturely for his age or enjoys

playing with younger children rather than children the same age or older, chances are he is suffering from a lack of self-confidence, low self-reliance, and low self-esteem. Playing with younger children relieves the child of the anxiety of living up to the standards or interests of his age group, while it simultaneously permits him to be more creative in his play. In releasing himself from expectations, he is free to do what he wants to do, whether or not it is appropriate to his age or advances his skills. There is, of course, a negative side to this, especially if your child plays with younger children because he's afraid he won't be accepted by his peers. Additionally, a child who associates primarily with younger children may be subject to negative social stigmas and suggestions about his capabilities.

For example, even as a fourth grader Barbara seemed to lack confidence and initiative. When given an assignment in class, she would always be first to raise her hand for help right after the assignment had been explained and demonstrated. Even after the teacher had gone over the work for her again, Barbara often was still unable to complete the assignment. Frustrated, her mother sought therapy.

It became clear that though Barbara was the oldest of three sisters, she clung to the role of baby in the family. Her younger sisters dominated her. In speaking of her daughter, her mother insisted that Barbara had always been a sensitive child.

Barbara's dependence was encouraged by her parents' expectations, attitudes, and actions. In the initial therapy session with her mother, the child was excessively shy and whiny. She clung to her parents with more than the usual apprehension about strang-

ers and new situations that would be suitable for a
child of her age, and her mother encouraged her
regressive behavior. Her father, a businessman who
traveled frequently, had failed to notice that Barbara
was no longer a baby. He still addressed her by baby
names like *Babbs* and *Tootles*. She was not allowed
to help with anything around the house or even
make rudimentary decisions about what clothes to
wear; her mother laid them out for her the night
before. If Barbara tried to help with such simple
tasks as setting the table, her father would intervene
saying, "No, baby; those plates are too heavy for you.
Let me do it. You sit down and don't strain yourself."
Even tying her shoes was something her father delighted in doing for her, rather than allowing her to
do it herself. Regardless of there being two smaller
children in the family, Barbara's parents still treated
her like the baby.

In this case, family therapy was imperative. In addition to her mother and father, Barbara's younger
sisters came to therapy sessions. A system of negoti-
ating and establishing contracts among the sisters
was worked out, including the use of toys and helping with chores around the house. Since Barbara was
the oldest, she was put in charge of making the
household chart and rotating the different chores
among the sisters. The jobs included feeding the
dog, taking out the trash, setting the table, helping
with after-dinner cleanup, and folding clean laundry.
Certain tasks were reserved for Barbara, since she
was the oldest—such as scrubbing the toilet and
shoveling the horse stall.

Fulfilling these contractual obligations, maintaining chore charts, and helping around the house helped Barbara begin to develop confidence and self-reliance. As she progressed, her parents were encouraged to allow her to stay up a half-hour later at night, since she was the oldest, and to award her additional privileges. Her father took her out alone for special times, such as shopping. With no additional provisions and no school-specific intervention, Barbara's academic performance improved as a result of increased self-esteem and self-reliance. She no longer felt helpless to do assignments and did not sit waiting for someone to do the work for her.

An Underachiever May Neglect Physical Appearance

A child who neglects his appearance may be suffering from low self-esteem. Studies have shown that physical attractiveness influences people's expectations of another's behavior, which in turn affects that behavior. Further, there is a relationship between self-esteem and physical attractiveness. Not only do physically attractive people have a higher self-esteem, but people with higher self-esteem take better care of their appearance. This is, of course, not to say that all people who are good-looking have high self-esteem, or that individuals who do not care especially for fashion or who neglect personal grooming suffer from low self-esteem. As with any judgment of this kind, use common sense. Appearance is merely another thing you should be aware of.

Steve was a ten-year-old, overweight child, who, although not academically talented, showed great prowess in drawing and other forms of artistic expression. Unfortunately, Steve had an overbearing father, who didn't believe in providing emotional reinforcement for his children—what we call the *warm fuzzies* of praise and affection. His father seemed to be always on the lookout for the opportunity to catch Steve doing something "bad." And it was his habit to yell his complaints across the room: "What do you mean you left your homework assignment in school?" or "The poor dog would starve if it were up to you to feed her." Steve would visibly shrink when his father yelled at him, and then he would go off and find something to eat.

Through therapy, Steve's father was made to recognize the positive aspects of Steve's behavior and to stop being such a perfectionist regarding his son. He was taught to praise Steve when he did something right and to ignore the times when Steve's performance was less than optimum. Steve stopped overeating.

You should always remember that no one is perfect and search for opportunities in daily life to "catch your child in the act of being good." Children do not do well without praise; it's a strategy that should never be underestimated.

An Underachiever Frequently Has Few Social Relationships

Neglecting personal appearance is one aspect of a larger problem: a child's withdrawal from association with others. Research has shown that children (particularly in the midschool years, from eight to twelve years old) who are depressed use inappropriate ways to explain their actions—making excuses and perhaps lying. These children are more likely to be underachievers and to display helpless behavior in school. Without professional help, such children will likely become more helpless and more withdrawn.

● *An underachiever may also develop the wrong friendships.* Even young school-age children form strong emotional ties with troublemakers as a means to "join the gang." This is more common in older children, when friendships and peer pressure become more pronounced. It is usually not possible, or advisable, to keep your child from forming such friendships. If the situation persists and the child clearly violates family values, it may represent something more than a simple exploration. In such cases, get help. With young children, however, if the problem is reasonably minor, a change of classroom might improve in-class behavior and academic performance. (For a more complete discussion of children and peer groups, consult the companion book *Helping Your Child Cope with Peer Pressure.*)

In evaluating your home environment for factors that may cause underachieving behavior, consider the following five factors. They are symptoms of underlying problems you should be aware of.

● *Emotional Problems*—Often a sudden drop in a child's achievement occurs when parents get divorced or some other severely traumatic upheaval takes place. Sometimes the child uses failure to achieve in school as a means of avenging himself on one parent or both, while at the same time avoiding direct responsibility for his poor academic performance. Only when the cause of the emotional disturbance is addressed and the child can freely discuss his anger or sadness (or whatever the emotion may be) can he resume normal performance in school.

• *Teacher Troubles*—Children often complain about their teachers, but if changes in academic performance accompany such complaints, you should look into the situation. Some complaints will definitely be legitimate. As much as we would like to believe teachers can handle the variety of children in their charge, genuine mismatches—in teaching and learning styles or in personality—do sometimes occur. Getting to know what happens in your child's classroom and meeting the teacher is part of taking an active role as a parent. Teachers usually welcome parental concerns. If, after looking into continual complaints and discussing the situation with your child and the teacher, there does seem to be a problem, a transfer to another classroom may resolve the matter. Be sure, however, that this does not become a pattern—that teacher troubles do not become the blanket excuse for poor performance.

• *Fear of Failure*—This is a complicated issue, described by the question, "If I don't try, how can I really fail?" This is a defensive measure—referred to as *affected apathy*—that your child may adopt in response to continual failure or even mediocrity. "Why should I work hard and only get a C?

Does this mean I'm stupid?" Rather than accept such a situation, underachieving children may resort to failing on purpose. Another scenario might involve the youngest child in a family having to cope constantly with older, more knowledgeable siblings. The child may find competing within the family oppressive, to say nothing of having to live up to the standards set by older brothers and sisters in school.

Take Sam, for example. His mother was a holdout from the hippie era, a woman from the sixties who came to therapy bragging about the IQ of her son and complaining that the child's teacher was "just too dumb" to understand him. She maintained that Sam made no mistakes in any of his homework and said that she failed to understand why Sam was not promoted into the next level of reading, spelling, and math. A conference with Sam's teacher indicated that Sam indeed made no mistakes, but he also completed few problems—which means that he had not adequately mastered reading, spelling, and math.

Both Sam's teacher and his mother were instructed in the need for Sam to overlearn. Even when the child could complete an assignment within a reasonable amount of time with perfect accuracy, he was required to complete another that attacked a similar problem. Needless to say, Sam showed considerable improvement in a short period of time, and he lost his fear of failure.

● *Brighter Paradox*, that is, when an especially gifted child falls behind in school—when this occurs, everyone involved becomes perplexed. Boredom is often the excuse, but similar to the syndrome of teacher troubles, this too may be cover for something else. New activities such as music, art, computers, or intellectually challenging games can provide the kind of high-level stimulation not ordinarily available in the classroom.

It is important for you to distinguish between simple boredom and signs of more severe depression; unfortunately they manifest themselves in much the same way. Symptoms over a period of two weeks or more should be taken as a sign of depression and help should be sought. A child who is unresponsive in class, who does not complete homework assignments, and who withdraws from the teacher and his classmates will need help from a professional.

Tony was a bright and attractive ten-year-old whose teacher referred him to therapy because of chronic problems with poor academic performance as well as thumb sucking, bed wetting, and poor social development. To assess the degree of Tony's problems, it was necessary to engage the entire family in therapy. His father was a brilliant and successful architect, and it became obvious that Tony was very close to his mother but distant from his father, who was angry at Tony for his failure to achieve in school. Because Tony's father was frequently out of the home and had little idea of his son's talents and capabilities, he was often critical of him and tended to negate the child's interests and abilities. Testing indicated that Tony was actually a very bright child whose talents, however, were not in the area of art and creativity but in math and science. Tony's father expected that Tony would perform as well in art related subjects as he had.

Urged by the therapist to try to understand his son

more and to release his very specific goals for Tony's success, Tony's father began to give the boy more leeway. He was taught to praise Tony's success in the subjects Tony liked and to respect the boy's natural aptitudes. It took some time, but Tony's father was eventually made to understand that he was actually inhibiting Tony by forcing him into areas he didn't relate to or have proficiency in. Tony's lack of progress and socially unacceptable behavior were cries for help.

This is often the paradox for very bright children. Unfocused and misunderstood, they are often labeled exactly what they are not—unteachable, unmotivated social outcasts—because they don't relate to the level of instruction or the content of what is being taught. The result is that they often drop out of the classroom situation. This is usually because they are bored; teachers unfortunately take the boredom for lack of intelligence, figuring that the reason the child doesn't participate is because he can't.

● *Peter Pan Syndrome*—Some children simply do not want to grow up. Quite often this problem arises around the fourth grade. At age eight, nine, or ten, childhood development takes a jump; we expect children to become more responsible both in schoolwork and in interpersonal relationships, as they begin to form their first long-term friendships. If this doesn't happen, it may indicate that a child is having difficulties. Parents often cooperate with their child's retreat. They are overprotective, rescuing the child and controlling his behavior. Your child may display symptoms of helplessness when doing his schoolwork, asking for excessive help on even rudimentary assignments. A parent must be careful to resist this kind of backsliding on the part of the child, while at the same time not dropping their parental supports too suddenly. A child's anxiety level may rise just as suddenly. It is best to introduce a child gradually to independence. If this is a problem with your child, the advice given to Barbara's parents and the strategies they implemented might help him resist the temptation to fall back into overdependence.

On the other hand, parents and teachers can often inadvertently foster this reaction from a child. This may often happen because parents feel the child is acting too old for his age and will not fit in with his social group or because the teacher simply does not have time to meet the individual needs of such a child. Nancy, for example, was a very bright child. She wanted meaning from what she did in school and refused to be a rote learner. She had a great deal of innate intelligence that helped her in her reading. Nancy also understood the physical and social world around her and had a good grasp of the English language. She loved to take part in adult conversations, even though she was only eleven. She knew the correct order of words and the meaning of a great many words, but most of all, she had an ability to apply what she learned—an ability that usually comes at a later age than Nancy's.

Unfortunately, Nancy had a teacher who accepted only word recognition as a reading skill and did not encourage Nancy to incorporate her own background in her reading. Nancy's work began to slip, and she began to withdraw from her teacher and classmates. She became introverted and depressed. Nancy's parents became concerned about her behavior and decided to speak with her teacher. A program was initiated that made Nancy's teacher aware of and more comfortable with Nancy's particular abilities. Her parents were encouraged to allow Nancy to expand on her reading at home and to employ tactics like making educated guesses at unknown words and to allow logical substitutions for unknown words. Soon Nancy was moving forward again, and the teacher had learned a valuable lesson in how to deal with a bright child.

Another critical factor in children's school performance is age. This is quite subtle and not entirely understood, but research from other countries sheds some light on the subject. From Spain, for example (Ferrer and Musitu), we learn that there is indeed a correlation between the grades children receive and their relative academic standing within their age group. Older children in the study did in fact perform better. Another study in Germany (Sticker) looked at children who were late entering school and were being held back. A child's slow progress was found to be more connected with the time parents spent with their babies and other postnatal factors than with prenatal influences, such as poor nutrition before birth.

Experts are aware that more recent studies have shown that taller children score slightly better on IQ tests. As with physical attractiveness, these results, however, relate more to testers' and teachers' expectations than to actual intelligence. The study concluded that big children seem more like adults and so are given the benefit of the doubt and allowed more response time. Sex roles may also influence teacher and parent expectations, which in turn affect how a child's performance in school is interpreted. Boys generally perform better in math, girls in reading; but this is due more to society's expectations than to some real difference between the sexes. We will say more on the effects of expectations on a child's achievement in Part Three and in our discussion of *positive reinforcement* and *feedback*.

READING: A BASIC SKILL AND AN INDICATOR OF UNDERACHIEVEMENT PROBLEMS

In many ways, your first concern about your child's scholastic competence should be reading ability. The extent to which your child masters this basic skill will affect his performance not only for the remainder of his academic career but for the balance of his life. A fluent reader is a good thinker, will write better, will have a larger vocabulary, and will generally be able to express himself better.

Thus children achieving significantly below the expected reading level for their age group are in jeopardy. There is a definite tendency among underachieving children to spend a minimum of time improving their reading skills. Educational research has shown, however, that simply by spending additional time reading—so-called "free reading"—virtually anyone can improve performance on tests of basic reading skills—vocabulary, spelling, and especially comprehension.

Adults overlook the complexity of the act of reading. For a young child, first making sense of this process called reading is not easy. It seems next to miraculous, when you consider the complexities involved, that anyone learned to read or write at all. Appreciating a little of what reading is about will aid you in helping your child through tougher parts of learning.

There are two basic approaches to teaching reading: the *phonics* method, known also as the "look-say" approach, by which words are orally sounded out, sound by sound, syllable by syllable; and the *whole word* method, which involves word recognition and association of a particular set of sounds with a pattern of letters on the page. These methods complement each other; good readers ultimately employ both, though often only one or the other is formally taught in the classroom.

In his article on teaching strategies, Brian Enright outlines some practical suggestions that can enhance a child's beginning reading. His recommendations basically employ the whole word method. Enright maintains that it is essential for a beginning reading teacher (and why not a parent?) to put together a set of "sight words"—words a child knows by sight, not by sounding them out. These words are to certain "number facts" in arithmetic and can be considered the foundation of a child's fluency at figuring out print. Words that occur frequently in children's primers but are not easily sounded out are best presented in this way.

English is not a particularly phonetic language and requires learning by rote to associate certain sounds with specific words. The word *sight* itself provides an example; the way it appears in print (orthography) differs radically from its pronunciation—the sound we must "hear" in our minds and associate with meaning in order to make sense. An estimated 40 percent of our language has this difference between spelling and sound, which makes it difficult for a child to learn strictly by sounding out words.

Lists of sight words can beef up a weak reader's recognition vocabulary and so increase reading fluency. Children learn to understand and use spoken words before they can read, which means that a poor reader may have a normal or larger speaking vocabulary. Only the inability to make the connection between those printed marks and the sounds he understands and uses prevents him from reading well. For a further discussion of reading strategies, consult the companion book *How to Be a Good Role Model for Your Child*.

Be hopeful. Above all, the underachieving child should not be the focus of criticism and negativity in your family. Learning in school is difficult enough for any child, and the underachiever needs that much more support from his family. As a parent, you must take the initiative and provide love, support, and encouragement for all your children. If your underachiever is an exception, he must be handled in an exceptionally positive manner. In the next part, we offer some basic strategies and specific methods for helping your child to improve.

Part III
Specific Strategies
to Help Your
Underachiever

There are two classic strategies for directly helping an underachieving child: the educational
and the psychological. The educational strategy involves tutoring in the academic areas the child needs
help with, using teaching methods that address the
child's dysfunction. The psychological strategy ad-
dresses mental and emotional factors that may pre-
vent a child from performing to his potential. A combination of these approaches usually proves most
effective, because true underachievement may be
caused by a combination of psychological, social,
and learning disorders.

In implementing the following specific strategies,
always remember that a solid family base is your
child's most valuable asset in a fluctuating world. To
be effective, your family must function as a unit. The
whole is greater than the sum of its parts, though

this depends on each part working well both indi-vidually and as part of the whole. What happens with one member of the family, be it you, your spouse, or one of the children, profoundly affects both how the group works together and how each member can perform on his own. The home—more than school or any other influence—is the key factor in your child's academic achievement. You should consider whether your home environment and lifestyle are conducive to studying, whether reading materials are available, and whether TV watching is con-trolled. More important and more complex is the emotional atmosphere of your home and family dy-namics. How do you and your child interact? Do you engage in activities that resemble good study habits, such as reading? Do you carry on conversations with your child about subjects studied in school? Do you take an interest in your child's studies? Consider these questions as you implement the following strategies.

HELPFUL HINT #1—GIVE YOUR CHILD MORE RESPONSIBILITIES AS HE GROWS

To foster responsibilities in your child—which is what you should do—be sure to choose tasks appro-priate to his developmental capacities; even a four-year-old, for example, can help set the table. A number of factors are known to enhance children's willingness to try new tasks and to encourage gains in self-esteem and self-reliance:

● Assign tasks appropriate to your child's limits. That is, don't expect a five-year-old to accomplish such tasks as budgeting his weekly allowance.

● Help your child with a task before he is on his own. Let the child observe you, try the task with you, then do it while you watch and encourage him. Follow these steps at least once before the job becomes part of the child's routine.

● Remember that repeated demonstrations and loving supervision with encouragement are often necessary for the first few times your child attempts a new task.

● Do not hold your child to adult standards. This is an obvious caution, but all too often it is overlooked by anxious parents wishing to encourage their child's development.

● Give compliments and express appreciation. When you comment at all on your child's performance, *make it a positive remark*. This requires you to look and see what the child has done right. "Catching people when they do something right" is a better way to ensure more correct behavior than to point out where they went wrong.

● Do not smother your child's enthusiasm by going over procedures once he has completed the job. This communicates dissatisfaction with the results and may have a negative effect, fostering dependence on you for cures and step-by-step approbation, rather than building self-confidence and self-reliance.

● Do not give your child additional tasks just to keep him busy and out of the way, or as punishment. Motivation for work bogs down if tasks seem endless. Your child's feeling of being overburdened may foster the depressing notion that his work is never done and may destroy his motivation.

● Most of all, be patient and generous with your encouragement. Try not to exaggerate, however, as you are modeling responses for your child. In regard to being a good model, a number of expert suggestions are contained in the companion volume *How to Be a Good Role Model for Your Child.*

For an underachiever, learning *how* to work is more important than the social value or proficiency of the task. For the unmotivated or unproductive child, the challenge is mastering the following steps: (1) taking the initiative; (2) following through; (3) making positive associations with the completed work.

Added to these general recommendations, you should be aware that your choice of tasks for your child and their content have strong implications for sex-typing. Girls should have opportunities to manipulate mechanical devices and work with tools. Boys should know how to set tables and do dishes and laundry. You will do your children a great favor in allowing them a variety of household experiences.

HELPFUL HINT #2—PROVIDE MOTIVATION THROUGH ENCOURAGEMENT

Positive feedback reinforces your child's productive behavior. Children have to learn through experience what brings them academic success. Strictly speaking, *feedback* merely informs the child what he is doing right. *Praise* bridges the gap between the act and motivation. For best effect, praise should be specific—directly associated with a particular behavior—and descriptive. You might say to your child when he has done a homework assignment, "I love it when you do your homework and bring it to me all finished, just like this. I know you are working at your studies, and it makes me feel proud. Let me give you a hug." This kind of praise provides concrete information to the child about what he should do— what he has in fact just done and can continue to do—in addition to providing warmth and attention.

Many educators recommend using a more concrete reward system than praise or mere positive expression. Possible practices vary and should be evaluated with consideration of your child's interests. One common technique is a token economy. Under this scheme, your child scores points based upon specific academic performance. These points may be cashed in for prizes or rewards. A child may elect to cash in points on a weekly basis for lower-priced rewards, such as a trip to the ice skating rink or TV privileges. Or the child may prefer delayed gratification leading to bigger rewards, like horseback riding lessons or a new cassette player. The token system has advantages in that it teaches basic economic principles while motivating the child to perform academically. There are, however, doubts as to whether this method will lead children to establish good study habits and sufficient self-motivation that will persist throughout formal schooling without extrinsic rewards. Keeping in mind that scholastic success independent of token rewards and good academic behavior are the eventual goal, the token economy can work as an *initial* strategy to turn some underachievers around.

If you choose to use the token economy, you should not use it without praise. Praise and adult approval in general provide positive feelings your child will take to heart. Eventually these feelings will become part of a sense of self-satisfaction with work well done, and your approval will no longer be the prime motivation. The same thing will not necessarily happen with horseback riding lessons. Therefore, whatever system you use, also employ generous amounts of positive reinforcement. The academic and personal benefits of increased self-esteem from such simple measures will pleasantly surprise you.

The key in fostering motivation and productive study behaviors is setting appropriate goals. This is overlooked as often as specific praise for specific behavior. As with any training process, goals you set must take into account your child's current behavior. Goals should also be compatible with his skill level. The ultimate goal may be several weeks, months, or years away, but you should establish interim goals with definite, verifiable behaviors. It is easier to work toward a specific, attainable goal than to work just for work's sake. If the first goals are only small positive steps, the proper momentum to sustain later, more challenging leaps will nevertheless be begun and will be enhanced as your child experiences continued success.

You should always involve your child in establishing the expected goals. Sit down together and carefully go over his or her current capabilities and present problems. Allow the child to express emotions and frustrations before the process of problem solving and goal setting begins. Identify some specific objectives, soliciting input from the child. Write the goals down—have the child do the actual writing, if he is able—and then decide what goals seem most immediately appropriate and in what time frame. You may want to break down the goals further into easier, more attainable objectives. This goal-setting process directly models decision making where adults determine realistic goals and objectives for their lives. You also gain the child's confidence by involving him in goal setting, thereby increasing his willingness to comply with the terms you agreed on together.

Once you and your child have established goals, you might post a list of the major goals and the means used to accomplish them on the refrigerator or some other prominent place in the house. A checklist could be set up. Each time a specific goal has been met, or if the goal is an ongoing behavior— say, studying spelling every night of the week for

Friday's test—take the opportunity to praise your child for both achieving the goal and for the specific act of studying. You might want to have weekly or bi-weekly meetings—depending, of course, on the time frame or stage of the goal-setting process—to monitor progress and provide an opportunity for praise. If you make these meetings a positive experience and are supportive, your child will develop a positive attitude toward goal setting and the whole process of working in school.

Again, it's important that you focus attention on the positive. If your child does not succeed at step number one or has trouble achieving the first objective, identify something he has done right. Even the initial act of sitting down with you to set goals is a positive step. Say as much. If nothing else happens, mention enthusiastically how proud you are that you have agreed to meet together, that the child has identified a problem and has helped set specific goals toward solving it. Be sincere.

From a strong base of positive reinforcement, you can then start again: ask your child how it seems to be going; have the objectives been achieved? No? What went wrong, when, and where? Maybe new, less difficult, or simply more specific goals have to be set. Talk it out; the process can be slow. Be patient. Encourage what results you do see, and most of all, don't give up if the first efforts don't meet with instant success. *Remember that most children, and especially underachievers, must overlearn.* This may try your patience at first, but if you stick with it, you will eventually incorporate it in your expectations and your routine. Continue to meet and monitor progress, setting new goals when necessary. As your child becomes more capable, the less time each task will require for completion. Just meeting with the child may have positive effects in the long run.

When Barbara's parents realized, for example, that their habit of treating her as a much younger child was unhealthy and actually inhibited her progress, they sat down with her and made up a list of tasks around the house that Barbara could accomplish. They mutually agreed on those Barbara was interested in doing. As she mastered the routine of the first level of chores and both she and her parents were happy with her progress, they met again to determine what her next set of tasks might be. Working together on this progress meant that Barbara's parents had a better idea of what their daughter was capable of and provided the acknowledgment of what Barbara had set out for herself.

The basic idea here is that nothing succeeds like success. The experience of succeeding provides your child with real motivation to do more. Success *feels* good. You can tell your daughter to try harder or get organized, but until she learns specifically what that means and that she is capable of doing these things, she will not internalize your advice. But even before she takes specific actions, she has to understand why she should work. By praising, you communicate the rewards of success, giving the initial impetus to your child's efforts.

Remember Larry and his timed math drills? The first two times, neither Larry's attitude nor his progress was very good, but due to positive encouragement, something apparently clicked in his mind about what was expected of him and why he ought to do it. Other students also were timed at division problems. Larry was by no means the fastest, but he understood what he had to do to progress and why. Larry's parents worked with him nightly, timing his progress. The results were directly measurable and he immediately understood them, both in terms of seconds shaved and number of problems answered correctly. Larry got faster. He worked harder and asked for other such challenges. Though he was not the fastest or most accurate in class, he found something of interest to talk about with other students. And since he worked at it, his progress was far more marked than that of most students.

The teacher posted the results of these timed exercises at the students' request. Week by week Larry moved up in the class rankings. As he realized that he could accomplish goals, he began working at other things for school. He was interested in doing well on the timed mathematics exercises, and because other students were also interested in how he did, Larry also became involved in other assignments and activities other students were doing in school. The breakthrough for Larry was more than just academic; he learned that he could succeed socially in school with a little effort and by taking interest in activities. Larry had it in him to improve all along. He might have made progress on timed math exercises without any help. It was, however, the precise feedback and positive reinforcement that changed Larry's attitude. If his parents and teacher had not used the stopwatch and brought his progress to Larry's attention, he might have learned nothing more than

math, if that—and little about his ability to succeed
or why he ought to care about success. Needless to
say, Larry felt better about himself and learned that if
he cared, others would care also. He learned that if
he tried, he could succeed—and that success feels
good.

HELPFUL HINT #3—MAKE READING A PRIORITY

Reading ability is in one respect like shoe size: children need to read books that fit their ability. If a
book is too easy for your child, not only will he not
be learning, but the practice of reading will seem
constricting. He may become bored and inattentive,
compounding rather than improving his problems.
On the other hand, if the book is too advanced—at
what is referred to as the frustration level—a weak
reader will feel overwhelmed. Not only will the
child quickly become tired without retaining much
of what has been read, but he will not want to read
and will resist you.

A book to be used for teaching reading must be
just right, with a little room for growth. To find out
what your child's reading ability is, get some books
from the library that are below, at, and above the
child's grade level. Have your child casually read sec-
tions to you out loud, with no one else around. If
about 10 percent of the words on a given page are

unfamiliar and can't be read by the child, the book is too difficult to enjoy. If 2 percent or less of the words per page can't be pronounced, the book is good for instructional purposes. If your child can read smoothly with practically no mistakes, the book is at the recreational reading level. When the child stumbles over a word during this session, just say the word correctly; at this point you are only assessing his skills, and actual instruction does not enter into the process.

It may be that your child's reading level is well below his age or grade level. This can cause problems of interest; a twelve-year-old will hardly feel motivated to read *The Cat in the Hat* if the book is embarrassingly difficult. To find the right book may take a bit of thought after trying a few for readability. Your child's teacher may be of some assistance, or perhaps there is a reading specialist or resource person in your child's school. Another alternative, if you have the time and inclination, is to write your own stories using a carefully limited vocabulary and sentence style. Typing these is, of course, helpful. Your local school may even have a large-print typewriter you can use. Even telling anecdotes or making up stories together can benefit your child, especially older children with a rudimentary grasp of reading.

Other things to keep in mind when selecting a book for readability are: sentence length; basic vocabulary of the test; frequency of difficult or long words, or words unfamiliar to the child; and how often new ideas are presented and how complex they are. You should also watch for figures of speech and complicated modes of expression, such as irony or metaphors; and, of course, appropriateness of subject or story.

The importance of subject matter is paramount. Include your child in selecting the kind of book he enjoys. Often a child will read remarkably better, with more focused attention and better comprehension, because he is interested in what's being read. The mental capacity is there. Your child just has to be drawn out to become engrossed in the act of reading.

A variety of research strongly supports the idea that reading aloud to your child can help him develop a positive attitude toward reading and enhance his competence. Additionally, when parents read to their children, some studies show an increase in both listening and speaking vocabularies, better letter recognition, and spoken sentence length. Comprehension is improved. Children who have been read to are also more likely to read on their own and seek out information and entertainment in books. Children whose parents read to them as few as four times per week for as little as eight to ten minutes each time will show greater enthusiasm for reading and achieve higher levels of competency than children who were not read to at home. Further, the same studies discovered that while children of average intelligence had parents who read to them about eight minutes a day, gifted children's parents read to them an average of about twenty minutes a day. Most research also indicates that children who talk more about stories and ask questions about reading end up with higher scores on comprehension and other reading tests. This is contrary to the notion that children should learn just to listen while a story is being read. Young children need to ask questions; doing so means they are engaged and trying to follow the details.

Give time for and encourage your child to ask questions about the story and what's going on. Even ask your own questions periodically, in a friendly, nonthreatening manner. This allows your child a chance to participate in the story and lets you check to see whether your child is engaged or if it's time to put the book aside.

Questions should be varied and concern specific words and details of the story. Also ask questions about what may happen next. For example, in those places in any story where a choice has to be made, ask your child, "What do you suppose is going to happen now?" Let him tell you, and allow for a full response.

Ask about details previously in the story—things your child asked about or that you pointed out. In these exchanges, also try to use the new vocabulary in the story to talk about what's going on. If, for example, the story involves words or objects unfamiliar to your child, explain what the thing is, what it's used for in the story, and point to the word. Have the child spell it out or write it out. Later, at some turn in the plot, when you ask the child about what will happen, ask about that subject, if it's pertinent. How will it figure in the story? You might keep a list of new words.

Primarily, though, the experience of being read to

should be fun. Questions and answers should be conversational and not a kind of third-degree interrogation. The objective behind your questioning is to model and encourage your child to ask questions and imagine on his own. This is true of TV watching as well. Understanding the details of what's happening in a story and speculating about what may happen next in print or on the screen are not natural activities. They have to be taught.

Another exercise sometimes used in schools asks the child to picture the scene as it's described in a story. Some observers have speculated that children growing up with large doses of TV and movie images being flashed at them may be unable to generate or express clearly in words the pictures in their imaginations. They are more likely to be suffering from a visual overload. It is even more difficult to get from print or spoken words a visual image of what's being described.

Parental expectations are very important to reading. If your child believes that you think he should succeed in reading, he will take reading seriously. This belief is communicated through two channels: your actions and your praise. If you set aside time to read both for yourself and to your child, he will see that reading does matter to you. When your child picks up a book, asked about reading, or achieves some small success in reading, praising the effort will also communicate that reading counts. When your daughter comes to you and says she has just started a story or has gotten a book from the library, you might say, "That's wonderful. I'm very happy you did that all on your own. Reading is very important."

You might also ask to see the book, look at it, read a little of it aloud. Ask questions and encourage your child to seek you out. You might also set aside time for family readings, with each person reading something aloud, or story telling from either actual or made-up events. At dinner and other times, talk about things you are reading or have read. Ask whether your child read anything interesting that day. You child will learn to be interested by seeing your interest.

Studies show that in households where a broad range of reading material (books, magazines, newspapers) is available, children are more likely to have a positive attitude toward reading and achieve better on reading tests. Therefore, keep as much reading material as possible around the house. You might also schedule trips to the library for you and your child to check out books.

As a final word of caution, try to avoid putting pressure on your child to read more or better, especially if he is an underachiever. Punishment is a definite mistake. The only way to ensure success at reading is for your child to develop a spontaneous, self-motivated reading habit, which requires positive associations with reading. Praise and good feelings then will further these ends. Badgering with threats or cross-examinations about what's been read are certainly counterproductive.

Use the following ten suggestions to increase your child's word recognition. As he becomes more adept, he will take greater pleasure in reading:

1. When an unfamiliar word occurs in your

child's reading, ask for educated—not wild—guesses about what the word is, or even about what it may mean. Often a child can (and should) learn to figure this out from the context.

2. Provide your child a chance to notice when he makes an error that what he has read does not make sense. Don't quickly supply the right word, but let the child work on it.

3. Accept logical substitutions—for example, *house* instead of *home*. This shows that the child is reading for meaning and is interpreting the print with a large degree of success. Eventually he will correct himself.

4. Rather than using lists and sounding out letters and individual syllables of words, have your child practice on longer passages. Reading flows in linguistic units. Don't underrate the motivational factor of an interesting story or subject. Alleged non-readers or poor readers are often capable of reading the entire sports section, including complex charts and graphs!

5. Don't confuse spelling with reading. Reading involves comprehension; spelling involves only memorization.

6. Don't confuse oral and silent reading. Oral reading is a type of performance—a skill separate from reading for meaning.

7. It's OK to read the entire story for the child beforehand. If you do, allow him to look at the text as you read along, perhaps using your finger to point to words as you read them. This enables him to become familiar with the test before attempting it, and also models what you expect.

8. Allow the child to point at the words while reading; it's OK.

9. Write out songs, chants, and nursery rhymes, so that your child can see what familiar litanies look like in print. He already knows the verses by heart; he will bring that comprehension to the reading.

10. Be tolerant of mistakes. Be patient and allow your child time to make his own corrections and go at his own pace. The absence of mistakes indicates knowledge is already there; too much ease may mean the text is below your child's reading ability and learning is not taking place.

HELPFUL HINT #4—MONITOR AND CONTROL TV; MAKE TV WORK FOR YOU AND YOUR CHILD

Much of what we recommend for reading also applies to TV. The only way to differentiate between good and poor TV shows is to actively watch, comprehend, and analyze what you see—similar to the process of appreciating what you read. It has been said, in the movie, *Reuben, Reuben*, "There is no trashy writing, only trashy readers." The idea is that all reading in itself is good and that only by first reading can you judge the relative merits of one book against another. The broader sense of the quote implies that any intellectual activity is better than being mentally lazy. In this sense, the statement applies to TV.

Though all TV shows may provide a basis for some kind of thinking, we recommend using discretion in selecting programs, especially in the case of under-achievers. Children who are having trouble in school—or anyone for that matter—should not watch TV at the expense of reading or other activities. Even family conversation should take precedence over TV watching.

Turn the set off during dinner, or better still, eat where there is no TV, to allow for family dialogue. The news can wait. If you're really concerned, tape the evening reports. Some astute family member once noted that the TV seemed to monopolize family conversation. No one seemed to talk so much at the dinner table and command such attention from everyone else—even during grace. Limit TV intake at meal times.

Tailor your child's TV watching to his age and developmental stage. Just as the book must fit the child, TV shows must also be appropriate to his age and understanding. If you feel unprepared to make such a decision, consult your child's teacher and other parents of children about the same age. As with reading, it helps if you can watch TV with your child. You can ask and answer questions; carry on a dialogue with the TV show. If you have a VCR, you might record certain shows so your child may view them several times. This is especially effective with some educational shows that present complex concepts in a short period of time. Don't underrate television as a learning tool.

HELPFUL HINT #5—CHECK OUT YOUR CHILD'S SCHOOL

In elementary school, your child encounters a great many influences. The teacher, other students, and the physical and social environment all combine to affect your child's performance in and out of school. Sometimes severe negative effects don't become apparent until the early teen years—the result of problems that could have been headed off at an earlier pass.

Follow these steps in assessing your child's academic surroundings:

1. Arrange to visit your child's class. Teachers will generally welcome your interest. If possible, also arrange for a post-visit meeting with the teacher, so you can ask questions about what you observed and get an understanding from the teacher's perspective.

2. Look at the physical arrangement of the room. Is it rigid, suggesting little opportunity for relaxed teacher-student and student-student interaction? Are the walls blank or covered with posters and student work? How is the furniture arranged? How do *you* feel in the room? If you have an opportunity to talk with the teacher after school, you might ask questions about the room arrangement and particular fixtures, to find out what kind of thinking went into the setup.

3. Sit where the teacher tells you, and watch

how he interacts with the students. How do the students respond to the teacher? What is the teacher's body language, both in general and in regard to certain students? Does he allow time for the students to respond? Are there obvious differences between how the teacher interacts with some students?

4. Notice the class size. A wide variety of studies targeting different areas of performance all point to one conclusion: the more time spent with each student engaged in a particular learning sequence, the better students master the instructional objectives. For the underachiever, usual approaches employed in schools today include tutoring, special class placement with fewer students, and individualized lessons with modified objectives and exercises for as long as needed. In fact, there is a movement in education toward individualized self-paced instruction. (Given current conditions in schools and the demands in education, however, it is doubtful that full individualization will ever be achieved.)

5. If possible, visit several different teachers' classrooms. In upper grade levels, you might observe a teacher during several periods to see whether there is a difference in how that teacher behaves with different groups. It need not be your child's class. In fact, seeing another class might prove more informative.

A 1979 study conducted by teacher Eigil Pedersen illustrates the graphic effect a teacher can have on children. Pedersen reviewed three hundred of his former students' files. One hundred eighty-seven of his students had one of three teachers, whom he labeled A, B, and C. Teacher A Pedersen classed as benevolent for having fostered a good feeling toward school and learning; B was neutral; and C had somehow caused negative feelings in the majority of students toward learning in school. The children had been given IQ tests in first grade and later in grades three through six. The difference among the groups of students who had teachers A, B, and C was obvious: 36 percent of students taught by A in first grade showed marked increases in IQ in later grades; B's students remained relatively stable; while 40 percent of C's students showed a decline and only 12 percent showed even small gains. Pedersen concluded from this evidence that the foundation for later progress had been laid—or undermined—in the students' earliest encounter with classroom learning.

Pedersen followed up on these findings in grades three through six to determine whether sex had any effect on how these same teachers and students responded to each other. Teacher A's effect seemed equally positive with both sexes, and teacher C was equally destructive. However, B's girls showed marked increases, while twice as many boys showed decreases. It seems that teacher B could hardly be called neutral.

Pedersen did not stop there. He investigated the adult status of these former students. He based his conclusions on such things as their occupations, income, housing quality (in terms of rent), and neighborhood. Then he divided his findings into three classes. Approximately two-thirds of A's former students were in the top third of adult status according to those indicators. None of Teacher A's students were in the bottom third. Former students of B and C were scattered among the three class categories, with the majority in the lowest rank. Teacher A's former students had done far better on average than either C's or B's. The study was performed after the fact and was not conducted scientifically. The students were not tracked according to ability. Thus we don't know whether teacher A had had all the brilliant students, or a larger share of students from wealthy families. Though it's impossible to isolate the cause for their success, it would seem more than a coincidence that so many of A's students did so well in comparison to B's and C's students.

CONCLUSION

"The child is the father to the man." How often have we heard that little truism? It is in the formative years, from birth to twelve years old, that a person's basic character is etched. This is the time of life that social, physical, and school-related skills are developed. It is through the many experiences your child has in this period of life that he learns a sense of competence or inferiority. The consequences of how your child performs have clear-cut implications for how he feels about himself and others. Can I compete? Can I find out what is important to me? Do I have the ability to satisfy my curiosity about things? Am I just as good as the other kids, or is what I do worse than what they can do? Will things always be this way?

The school is the first serious contact your child will have with the world outside his home. It is within its walls that your child must first learn the meaning of competition and how he will fare with others in this miniature marketplace. You must exert your influence upon the life of your child so that he will be able to compete successfully. The elementary school is a place of important influences on your child that will have profound effects in their immediate impact as well as in the long run.

You have the wherewithal to help your child succeed in school, and it is your responsibility to do so. Like all the other tasks of child rearing, it's an investment in time, energy, and emotion that is well worth making. A child who has been loved and nurtured in his first years at home will have a solid foundation with which to meet the demands made on him as he starts school—and during the rest of his life. There is no better time to start than now.

Other books in this series that may be helpful to you include *How to Be a Good Role Model for Your Child*, which emphasizes the effect of the family on child development, and *When Your Child Grows Up Too Fast*, which offers advice for helping children who have dropped out because they were pushed too hard, too fast.

REFERENCES

Enright, Brian. "Teaching Strategies." *Childhood Education*, November/December 1985.

Ferrer, Jesus, and Gonzalo Musitu (Colegio San Jose de Valencia, Spain). "Influence of the Age Variable in School Performance." (Span.) *Psicologica*, vol. 1 (2), pp. 207-214 (July 1980).

Garber, Howard L. "Bridging the Gap from Preschool to School for the Disadvantaged Child," *School Psychology Digest*, vol. 18, pp. 303-10 (1979).

Krouse, H., and Helene J. Krouse. "Toward a Multimodal Theory of Academic Underachievement." *Educational Psychologist*, vol. 16 (3), pp. 151-64.

Lowenstein, L. F. "Recent Research in the Identification, Prevention and Treatment of Underachieving Academic Children." *Community Home and School Gazette*, vol. 173 (6), pp. 243-46 (Sept. 1979).

Merton, Robert K. *Social Theory and Social Structure*, revised edition. New York: Free Press, 1957.

Pedersen, Eigil. "The Lifelong Impact of a First Grade Teacher." *Instructor*, vol. 89 (5), pp. 62-63, (Dec. 1979).

Rist, Ray C. "Student Social Class and Teacher Expectations: The Self-Fulfilling Prophecy in Ghetto Education." *Harvard Educational Review*, pp. 411-51 (1979).

Silvern, Steven. *Childhood Education*, September/October 1985.

Sticker, Elisaveth, J. (Reinische Freidrich-Wilhelms—U Bonn, Psychologisches Inst., West Germany). "Born Too Early—Disadvantageous for School Achievement?" (Germ.) *Psychologie in Erziehung und Unterricht*, vol. 32 (2), pp. 81-92. 1985,

Willerman, Lee. "Effects of Formulas on Intellectual Development." *American Psychologist*, vol. 34 (10), pp. 923-29 (Oct. 1979).